MW01643662

Inspired by CJ's example, this story teaches kids to embrace kindness, humility, and inclusion as they strive to make everyday count.

Marie Ferdinand-Harris

illustrations by Kashif Qasim

DEDICATION

In loving memory of our beloved son, CJ Harris. Your short but impactful journey in this world continues to inspire us with your joy, innocence, and resilience, reminding us to embrace every moment and face life's challenges with grace.

With deep gratitude and love, we remember those who shaped CJ's life journey: His loving dad, Cedrick Harris, his late maternal grandmother, Jeantilia Ferdinand, his paternal grandparents, Mike & Gail Harris, his brothers, Dontay Harris & Ace Harris, his dedicated teachers, coaches, and trainers, his caring aunts, uncles, and all those who left an indelible mark on his life.

Your boundless love, unwavering support, and countless sacrifices have been the bedrock of our strength and determination. CJ's memory lives on in our hearts, a testament to the preciousness of time and the enduring impact of love and support.

FOREWORD

CJ Harris was an extraordinary young man who left a lasting impact in his short life. CJ, despite his tender age of 14, left an enduring legacy that profoundly impacted those fortunate enough to have known and loved him.

His life beautifully exemplified the timeless wisdom that it's not the quantity of years that matter, but the quality of life lived within them. In his brief time, CJ filled his years with purpose and touched the hearts of both young and old who crossed his path.

Remarkably, he had even earned a scholarship to play both football and baseball at LSU, his cherished dream! Yet, amid his many accomplishments, he remained the kind of child any parent would be profoundly proud of.

This book is a heartfelt tribute to CJ's memory, with the hope that its words will inspire the children who read and listen, encouraging them to aspire to "BE LIKE CJ!"

HIS CHARACTER

CJ's remarkable humility and his unwavering kindness towards other children, particularly those with special needs, served as the driving force behind the creation of this book.

CJ was an energetic and bright 8th grader who had a deep love for sports, particularly baseball, football, and basketball. But what truly set him apart was his character.

CJ was a quiet kid, but his heart was enormous. Being around him was like experiencing pure love. He always had a warm smile, and he extended his friendship to everyone, without any regard for their background. He made sure that even the kids who weren't the most popular felt heard and valued.

Whether you played alongside him, coached him, shared a laugh, took a walk, or simply sat down with him, you couldn't help but be captivated by his warm and genuine spirit.

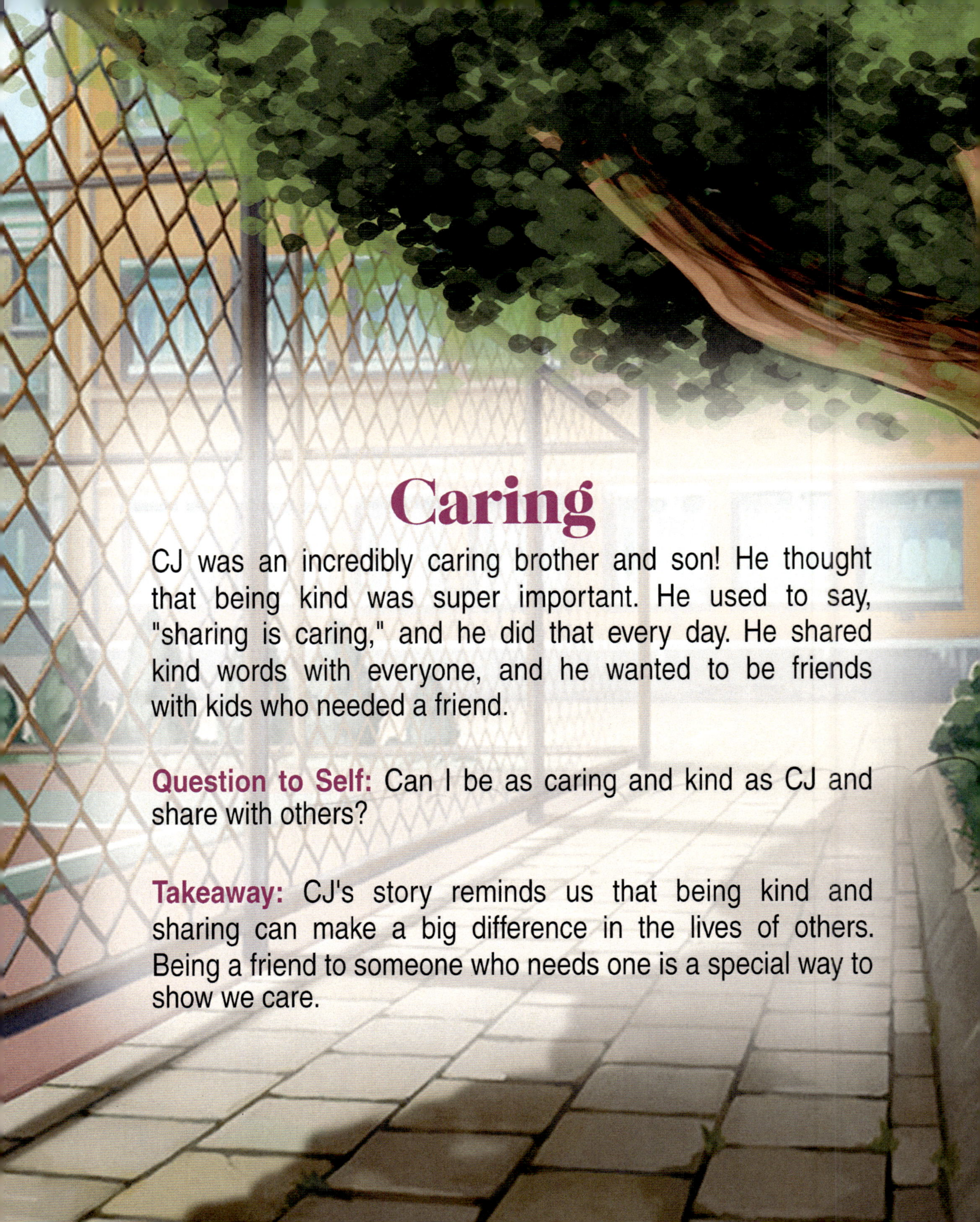

Caring

CJ was an incredibly caring brother and son! He thought that being kind was super important. He used to say, "sharing is caring," and he did that every day. He shared kind words with everyone, and he wanted to be friends with kids who needed a friend.

Question to Self: Can I be as caring and kind as CJ and share with others?

Takeaway: CJ's story reminds us that being kind and sharing can make a big difference in the lives of others. Being a friend to someone who needs one is a special way to show we care.

CJ
CJ
CJ
CJ
24

Ultimate Teammate

CJ was a true inspiration to everyone around him. He loved sports and cheered for his teammates. CJ had a willingness to help students struggling with sports. He wanted to inspire his teammates to believe in themselves. In every game, he did his best because he knew that if his team was winning by a lot, all his teammates would get a turn to play.

Question to Self: Can I be like CJ and be a good friend on the team and be nice when we play games?

Takeaway: CJ showed us that being a good teammate and making others feel great is a wonderful goal. Cheering for our friends and sharing the fun of sports can make everyone smile.

Special

CJ was special! What made CJ special was how he loved and helped kids who needed extra support, like those with disabilities or who didn't have enough clothes or food, or who were being teased. CJ would eat lunch with them and play games during playtime, and this made them super happy.

Question to Self: Can I be like CJ and be a good friend to kids who need extra love and help?

Takeaway: CJ shows us that being kind and helping others, especially those who might be going through a tough time, can make a big difference in their lives and make them smile.

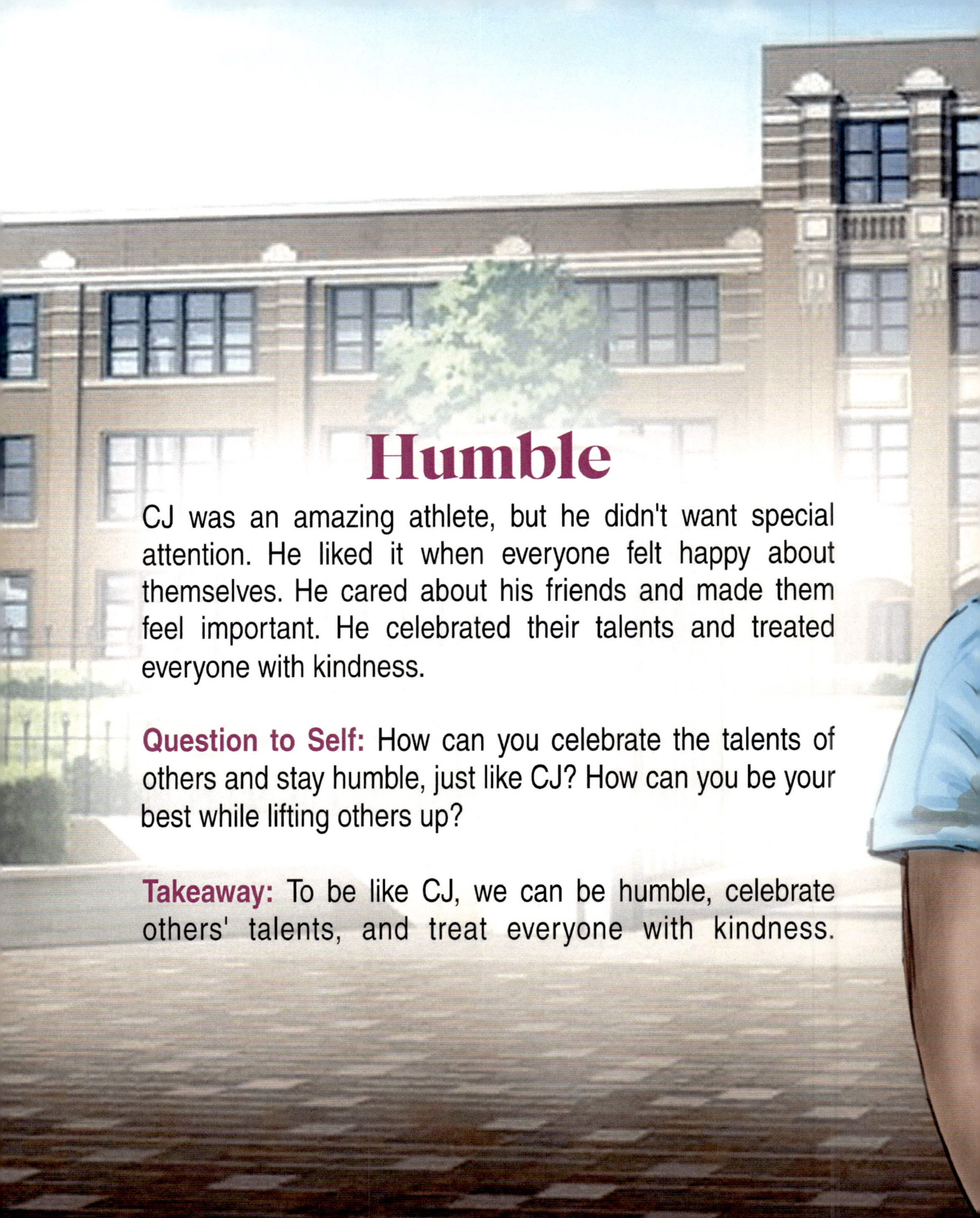

Humble

CJ was an amazing athlete, but he didn't want special attention. He liked it when everyone felt happy about themselves. He cared about his friends and made them feel important. He celebrated their talents and treated everyone with kindness.

Question to Self: How can you celebrate the talents of others and stay humble, just like CJ? How can you be your best while lifting others up?

Takeaway: To be like CJ, we can be humble, celebrate others' talents, and treat everyone with kindness.

THE AUTHOR

Marie Ferdinand-Harris, a Haitian American from a tight-knit family, draws inspiration from her mother's unyeilding spirit. She learned the values of perseverance, faith, and kindness from her upbringing. With a Bachelor of Science in Kinesiology from LSU, she's been honored with an induction into the LSU Sports Hall of Fame.

As the first Haitian in the Women's National Basketball Association (WNBA), Marie is a pioneer. Today, she serves as a motivational speaker and the Executive Director of the BeLikeCJ Foundation, which inspires children and families by offering programs that unite diverse backgrounds through service and sports.

Marie's debut children's book is inspired by her family, including her husband, standout athlete Cedrick Harris, and their son, CJ.

THE CJ STORY

On April 4, 2021, at the tender age of 14, CJ went home to be with the Lord following a tragic accident. CJ was born June 11, 2006, in Miami, Florida to proud parents Cedrick Harris & Marie Ferdinand-Harris.

CJ was a bright, 8th grade student at Ashdown Jr. High School in Ashdown, Arkansas. He was not your average fourteen year old.

CJ was a loving young man, exceptionally talented with a heart of gold. He was extremely kind- hearted and left a lasting impression on everyone he met!

THE BE LIKE CJ FOUNDATION

a 501(c)(3) organization

Our mission is to inspire children and families nationwide by uniting people of different backgrounds through service and sports programs.

You can be part of this remarkable movement by either volunteering or contributing financially. Simply go to our website, www.belikecj.org, and contribute to this amazing cause.

#BELIKECJ
FOUNDATION
belikecjfoundation.org
Follow us
BeLikeCJ Foundation

Made in the USA
Monee, IL
12 April 2025